Renal Diet Recipes

An Easy-to-Follow Guide with Delicious Low Sodium, Potassium and Phosphorus Recipes. Learn how to Stop Kidney Disease and Avoid Dialysis

Table Of Contents

Introduction

People with renal disease may need to take several essential nutrients and control their potassium, sodium, & phosphorus consumption. A renal diet cuts down the amount of waste in their blood resulting from drinks and food that are ingested. As kidney activity is affected, the kidneys do not adequately philter or extract waste. It will adversely influence the electrolyte levels of a patient if the excess is remaining in the blood. It can improve renal function and delay the development of total kidney disease by maintaining a renal diet.

An individual may delay or prevent some health problems due to chronic kidney disease (CKD) by eating healthy foods and avoiding foods high in sodium, potassium, and phosphorus. They must learn how to deal with calories, fats, proteins, and fluids. Protein foods, including beef and dairy goods, decompose into waste material eliminated from the blood by balanced kidneys.

Sodium is a (sodium chloride) mineral present in salt and is regularly used in food processing. Salt is one of the most often used seasonings; it requires time to become used to reduce the salt intake in your diet. Salt/sodium elimination, though, is a useful aid in managing renal disease.

Phosphorus is another mineral that will build up in the blood when your kidneys don't function correctly. Calcium may be extracted from your bones as something occurs and may settle in your blood vessels or skin. The bone disorder will then become a concern, making you too likely to get a crack in the bone.

Nutritional requirements shift as CKD advances. A health care professional can prescribe that foods be selected carefully by a person with reduced renal function. People often lose their appetites as CKD progresses because they figure out that foods do not taste the same. Consequently, they eat fewer calories and can lose too much weight, which are basic energy units in food. If they lose so much weight, renal dietitians may help people with advanced CKD discover healthier ways to incorporate calories into their diet.

An essential part of any eating plan is protein. Proteins help develop skin, muscle, connective tissue, bone, internal organs, and blood and maintain them. They help to combat illness and heal the wounds. But proteins also decompose into waste material, which the kidneys must expel from the blood. Consuming additional protein than the body requires will place excessive pressure on the kidneys and induce faster renal function deterioration.

Reducing potassium, phosphorus, & sodium consumption will be an essential part of treating the condition if you have kidney disease. The foods with high sodium levels, high potassium levels, and high levels of phosphorus mentioned above are possibly better restricted or avoided.

CHAPTER 1:

What Is a Renal Diet

The renal diet is a dietary regimen designed to convey respite to patients with deliberate or injured renal functions and chronic kidney diseases. There is no single type of renal diet—this is because requirements of the renal diet and restrictions need to match the patient's needs and be based on what the doctor prescribed for the patient's overall health.

However, all forms of renal diet have one thing in common: to improve your renal functions, bring some relief to your kidneys, and prevent kidney disease in patients with numerous risk factors, altogether improving your overall health and well-being. The grocery list we have provided should help you get hold of which groceries you should introduce to your diet and which groups of food should be avoided to improve your kidneys' performance, so you can start from shopping for your new lifestyle.

You don't need to shop for many different types of groceries all at once, as it is always better to use fresh produce. However, frozen food also makes a good alternative when fresh fruit and vegetables are not available.

Remember to treat canned goods as suggested and recommended in the portion and drain excess liquid from the canned food.

For the renal diet recommended in our guide, this form of kidney-friendly dietary regimen offers a solution in the form of low-sodium and low-potassium meals and groceries, which is why we are also offering simple and easy renal diet recipes. This dietary plan is compiled for all renal system failure stages unless the doctor recommends a different treatment by allowing or expelling some of the groceries that we have listed in our ultimate grocery list for renal patients.

Before we get to the cooking and changing your lifestyle from the very core with the idea of improving your health, you need to get familiar with renal diet basics to help you improve your kidney's health by lowering sodium and potassium intake.

Although there is no cure for CKD, this disease is completely manageable. Lifestyle changes can help slow the disease's development and evade symptoms that naturally begin to occur as the disease advances. These diet and regime variations can even advance your general health and help you manage associated conditions. When you begin making changes to your food and daily habits, you will also notice an improvement in these associated conditions, including hypertension and diabetes.

You can have a healthy, long, and happy life while managing this disease. Making proper changes early on can slow the progression of any adverse symptoms for several years. This will shed important light on you and your loved ones, so that together you can make positive changes that delay the progression of CKD for a long time to come.

Stage 1: Slight kidney damage, and usually no symptoms. (eGFR > 90 mL)

Stage 2: Mild damage in kidneys (eGFR = 60–89 mL)

Stage 3: Moderate damage in kidneys (eGFR = 30–59 mL)

Stage 4: Severe damage in kidneys (eGFR = 15–29 mL)

Stage 5: Kidney failure/End-stage CKD (GFR < 15 mL)

The Role of Phosphorous in Our Body

Phosphorous contributes to keep our bones healthy and develop them. Phosphorous helps in muscle movement, develops the connective tissue and organs. When we eat food that contains phosphorous, the small intestines store it to build our bones. A well-functioning kidney can get rid of the extra phosphorous in the body, but a damaged one cannot do so. So renal patients must watch how much phosphorous they are consuming.

Though phosphorous helps develop bones, it can also weaken the bones by extracting calcium from it if too much phosphorous is consumed.

The calcium removed from the bones gets deposited in blood vessels, heart, eyes, and lungs, causing severe health problems.

The proper knowledge of high phosphorous food is required to balance phosphorous for a renal patient. Red meat, milk, fast foods like burgers, pizzas, fries, fizzy drinks that are colored, and canned fish and seeds are relatively high in phosphorous.

Packaged food or canned food also, is high in phosphorous. Therefore, read the labels before you purchase any canned goods from the supermarket.

Phosphorous binders are an excellent way to keep your phosphorous intake to a minimum. If you ask you your dietitian, they will give you an excellent phosphorous binder, which you can follow to track how much you can and should consume.

Potassium

Potassium maintains the balance of electrolytes and fluids in our bloodstream. It also regulates our heartbeat and contributes to our muscle function. Potassium can be found in many fruits, vegetables, and meat. Besides, it also exists in our bodies. A healthy kidney keeps the required potassium in our body and removes the excess through urine.

A damaged kidney is not capable of removing potassium anymore. Hyperkalemia is a condition when you have too much potassium in the blood. Hyperkalemia can cause slow pulse, weak muscles, irregular heart rate, heart attack, and even death.

To control your daily potassium intake, count every ingredient's potassium level. It would help consult a renal expert dietitian, as they know which ingredient would work best for your condition. Food like avocado, beans, spinach, fish, bananas, and potatoes are very high in potassium. Even if you are eating these ingredients, try to divide the serving in half and eat a small serving.

Do not eat these high potassium ingredients every single day. There are many low potassium foods available. Pick them when you are making your meal plan. Fresh ingredients are always better than the frozen kind. To keep track of your potassium intake throughout the day, keep a personal food journal where you can input everything and reflect when you need to.

Sodium

A renal patient must cut down on daily sodium and potassium intake to keep their kidney at rest. Sodium and salt are not interchangeable. People have a misconception that salt is the only grocery item containing sodium, but other natural foods are high on sodium. Salt is a mixture of chloride and sodium. Canned foods and processed foods have a large amount of sodium in them.

Our body has three significant electrolytes, sodium, potassium, and chloride. Sodium regulates blood vessels and blood pressure, muscle contraction, nerve function, acid balance in the blood, and keeps the balance of fluid in the body! The kidney usually excretes the toxin in our body, but a damaged kidney cannot eliminate the extra sodium in our body.

So, when a renal patient consumes too much sodium, it gets stored in the blood vessels and bloodstream. This storage of sodium can lead to feeling thirsty all the time. It is a bit problematic, as a kidney patient must limit their fluid intake. It can cause edema, high blood pressure, breathlessness, and even heart failure. So, a renal patient must always limit their sodium intake. The average limit is 150 mg per snack and 400 mg per meal.

Patients who struggle with kidney health issues, going through a kidney dialysis, and having renal impairments need to go through medical treatment and change their eating habits and lifestyle to make the situation better.

The first thing to changing your lifestyle is knowing how your kidney functions and how different foods can trigger different kidney function reactions. Certain nutrients affect your kidney directly. Nutrients like sodium, protein, phosphate, and potassium are the risky ones. You cannot omit them altogether from your diet, but you need to limit or minimize their intake as much as possible. You cannot leave out essential nutrients like protein from your diet, but you need to count how much protein you are having per day. It is essential to keep balance in your muscles and maintaining a good functioning kidney.

A profound change in kidney patients is measuring how much fluid they are drinking. It is a crucial change in every kidney patient, and you must adapt to this new eating habit. Too much water or any other form of liquid can disrupt your kidney function. How much fluid you can consume depends on the condition of your kidney.

CHAPTER 2:

Types Of Food You Can Eat

Watching what you eat and drink is very important when you have chronic kidney disease. Before you enjoy the benefits of following a renal diet, you first must experience a mental makeover to break old, bad habits. The key to beginning the diet is thinking of it properly. Think of your goal as a healthier lifestyle, and remember that you want to stick to your renal diet for the probable future.

Now that you have a positive attitude, you need to give your pantry a makeover. Clean out your fridge and throw out expired food in your refrigerator and pantry.

Make time to do a list and concentrate on grocery shopping. A grocery list is an essential part of shopping and helps eliminate the guesswork. You tend to buy many things you don't need and spend a lot more money without a list. Spending enough time at the grocery store instead of rushing will allow you time to read the ingredient lists and nutrition labels.

Reading food labels is essential to making healthy food choices for your kidneys. When you have chronic kidney disease, you may need to limit some minerals and nutrients in your diets, such as sodium, phosphorus, and potassium. The amount of fat you eat should also be limited. The Nutrition Facts label will serve as a guide to help you make healthier choices.

Nutrition Facts

Serving Size ¼ cup (50g)
Servings per Container 18

Amount Per Serving	
Calories 300	Calories from Fat 110
	% Daily Value
Total Fat 12g	20%
Saturated Fat 4g	22%
Cholesterol 0mg	0%
Sodium 200 mg	8%
Total Carbohydrate 30g	10%
Dietary Fiber 0g	0%
Sugars 20g	
Protein 5g	
Vitamin A 5%	Vitamin C 0%
Calcium 10%	Iron 0%

* Percent Daily Values are based on a 2,000 calorie diet.

A well-stocked kitchen will ensure you have everything you need to cook and enjoy kidney-friendly meals, all while helping you feel better. Having healthy ingredients and snacks in your pantry and refrigerator will give you kidney-friendly nourishment all day long.

Below are some items that will help you create your grocery list for your next trip to the store. You don't have to buy everything on the list; instead, use this list as a guide for your kitchen staples. This list will help you find kidney-friendly goods at the grocery store that you can stock up on every month.

Grocery List for a Kidney-Friendly Pantry

Meat and Meat Substitutes

- Beef

- Chicken

- Eggs

- Egg substitute

- Fish

- Lamb

- Pork, chops/ roast

- Tofu

- Tuna, canned

- Turkey

- Veal

Vegetables

- Arugula

- Bean sprouts

- Cabbage, green/red

- Carrots

- Cauliflower

- Celery

- Chiles

- Chives

- Coleslaw

- Corn

- Cucumber

- Eggplant

- Endive

- Ginger root

- Green beans

- Lettuce

- Onions

- Parsley

- Radishes

- Turnips

- Vegetables, mixed

- Water chestnuts, canned

- Asparagus

- Beets, canned

Fruits

- Apples

- Blackberries

- Cherries

- Cranberries

- Figs, fresh

- Fruit cocktail

- Grapefruit

- Grapes

- Lemon

- Lime

- Peaches

- Pear

- Pineapple

- Plums

- Raspberries

- Strawberries

- Tangerines

- Watermelon

Bread and Cereals

- Bagels, plain/blueberry

- Bread, white/French/Italian

- Cereals, Kellogg's Corn Flakes

- Cereals, Cheerios

- Cereals, Corn Chex

- Couscous

- Crackers, unsalted

- Dinner rolls

- English muffins

Pasta

- Melba toast

- Rice, brown/white

- Noodles

- Oyste crackers

- Pita bread

- Tortillas

- Pretzels, unsalted

- Spaghetti

Fats

- Butter

- Cream cheese

- Margarine

- Mayonnaise

- Miracle Whip

- Nondairy creamers

- Olive oil

Sweets

- Animal crackers

- Angel food cake

- Candy corn

- Chewing gum

- Cotton candy

- Crispy rice treats

- Graham crackers

- Gumdrops

- Gummy bears

- Hard candy

- Hot Tamales candy

- Jell-O

- Jellybeans

- Jolly Rancher

- Lemon cake

- Life Savers

- Marshmallows

- Pie

- Pound cake

- Rice cakes

- Vanilla wafers

Beverages

- 7UP

- Coffee

- Cream soda

- Fruit punch

- Ginger ale

- Grape soda

- Hi-C

- Lemon-lime soda

- Lemonade

- Orange soda

- Root beer

- Tea

Dairy

- Almond milk

- Coffee-mate

- Mocha Mix

- Rice Dream

- Rich's Coffee

Other

- Apple butter

- Corn syrup

- Honey

- Jam

- Jelly

- Maple syrup

- Sugar, brown, or white

- Sugar, powdered

CHAPTER 3:

How Do Kidneys Work?

The kidneys are brown, weigh about 150 grams each, 12 centimeters long, 6 centimeters wide, and 3 centimeters thick. It is found in the body's dorsal wall on the spine's sides, upper part. Each kidney has an endocrine gland attached (it produces vital substances inside the body) called the adrenal gland.

The kidneys are the cleaners where the blood is filtered and cleaned. They produce urine, which contains water, toxins, and salts that the blood has been collecting throughout the body, and that has to be eliminated. They also intervene in other activities such as reproduction because they have sex hormones; regulate the amount of phosphorus and calcium in the bones; they control the tension in the blood vessels, and manufacture substances involved in blood clotting.

Renal insufficiency appears when only 5 percent of the total kidney or nephron filters work. The kidney's basic unit is the nephron, of which there are about 1 million in each organ. Each nephron forms a component that acts as a filter, the glomerulus, and a transport system, the tubule.

Some of the blood that reaches the kidneys is filtered by the glomerulus and passes through the tubules. Various excretion and reabsorption processes occur that give rise to the urine that is eventually removed.

The renal blood flow (RBF or amount of blood reaching the kidney per minute) is approximately adult 1.1 liters per minute. The 0.6 liters of plasma enter the glomerulus through the arterioles. The 20 percent is filtered, an operation called renal glomerular filtration.

Therefore, the renal glomerular filtrate is the volume of plasma filtered by the kidneys per unit of time. The amount of filtered plasma per day is 135 to 160 liters. To prevent fluid loss, between 98 percent and 99 percent of the renal glomerular filtration rate is reabsorbed by the tubules, resulting in the amount of urine removed from between one and two liters per day.

When a kidney disorder occurs, it means that one or more of the renal functions are altered. But not all functions are changed in the same proportion. If two-thirds of the nephrons cease to function, significant changes may not occur because the remaining nephrons adapt. Changes in hormonal production may go unnoticed. Then, renal glomerular filtration calculation is the only way to detect the decrease in the number of nephrons that continue to function.

Cause of Kidney Disease

Renal failure occurs when a disease or other health condition impairs kidney function, causing damage to the kidneys - which tend to worsen over several months and even years.

Diseases and conditions that usually cause chronic kidney disease include:

- Type 1 and 2 Diabetes

- Hypertension

- Glomerulonephritis, which is inflammation of the glomeruli, functional units of the kidneys where blood filtration occurs

- Interstitial Nephritis

- Polycystic Kidney Disease And Other Congenital Diseases That Affect Kidneys

- Prolonged urinary tract obstruction due to specific conditions such as prostatic hyperplasia, kidney stones, and some cancers

- Vesicoureteral reflux

- Recurrent renal infection is also called pyelonephritis

- Autoimmune Diseases

- Kidney injury or trauma

- Overuse of painkillers and other medicines

- Use of some toxic chemicals

- Kidney Artery Problems

- Reflux Nephropathy

Chronic renal failure leads to an accumulation of fluid and waste in the body. This disease affects most body systems and functions, including red blood cell production, blood pressure control, vitamin D levels, and bone health.

Risk Factors

Factors that are likely to increase a person's risk of developing chronic renal failure include:

- Diabetes

- Hypertension

- Heart diseases

- Smoke

- Obesity

- High cholesterol

- Be African American, Native American, or Asian American

- Have a family history of kidney disease

- 65 years or older

Chronic renal failure or uremia is the kidneys' inability to produce urine or fabricate low quality ("like water") since it has not been removed enough toxic waste. Although some patients continue to urinate, most cannot. However, the important thing is not the quantity but the composition or quality of the urine. Chronic kidney disease slowly worsens over time. In the early stages, it may be asymptomatic. The damage of function usually takes months to occur. When the person realizes, he is usually already with the functioning of the kidneys completely compromised. Early symptoms of chronic renal failure usually also frequently occur in other diseases and may be the only signs of renal failure until it is advanced.

Symptoms may include:

- General malaise and fatigue

- Generalized itching (itching) and dry skin

- Headaches

- Unintentional Weight Loss

- Loss of appetite

- Nausea

Other symptoms that may appear, especially when kidney function worsens, include:

- Abnormally light or dark skin

- Bone pain

- Drowsiness and confusion

- Difficulty concentrating and reasoning

- Numbness in hands, feet, and other body areas

- Muscle spasms or cramps

- Bad breath

- Easy bruising, bleeding, or bloody stools

- Excessive thirst

- Frequent hiccups

- Low level of sexual interest and impotence

- Interruption of the menstrual period (amenorrhea)

- Sleep disorders

- Swelling of hands and legs (edema)

- Vomiting, usually in the morning

CHAPTER 4:

How to Avoid Kidney Disease and Dialysis

Being diagnosed with chronic kidney disease is frightening, but you can take steps to keep away from dialysis when you discover the symptoms in the beginning. If you work intimately with your PCP, the odds are high you can, in any case, appreciate a refreshing personal satisfaction with kidney disease.

Following excellent health practices and evading dialysis, remaining at work, and understanding social exercises are ways individuals can feel responsible for their condition. Notwithstanding doing everything physically and medicinally conceivable to maintain a strategic distance from dialysis, having an occupation with medical coverage gives security that pays, and medical advantages will be accessible. Here are portions of the means to take to maintain a strategic distance from the beginning of dialysis;

Eat Right and Lose Excess Weight

Consistently make sure to know about serving sizes. It's what you eat that includes calories, yet also how much. As you get in shape, make sure to follow a smart dieting plan that consists of an assortment of nourishments.

Exercise

Most dialysis patients accept they can't work out. In all certainty, most dialysis patients can work out. Numerous renal patients depict regular exercise as the principal action that made them feel "normal" again after beginning dialysis medications. Regardless of whether it is just for a brief timeframe every day, movement allows the patient with persistent kidney disease to feel good, more grounded, and more responsible for their health.

Medicinal experts working in renal recovery have demonstrated that an ordinary exercise program, anyway restricted, not just upgrades an individual's potential for physical action, also improves the general personal satisfaction for individuals on dialysis. Exercise can also help the kidney symptoms patient recover the function to perform activities they were delighted in before being analyzed.

Try Not To Smoke

In case you smoke, there is, in all likelihood, no other choice you can make to help your health more than stopping. While an ongoing examination found that smokers lose ten years of life expectancy at any rate than people who never smoked.

Be Cautious of Glucose Levels

For good preventive health, cut back on soda pop, treats, and sugary baked goods, making glucose rise. If you have diabetes, this can hurt your heart, kidneys, eyes, and nerves after some time. Directing glucose is one of seven estimations for heart health, according to the American Heart Association. These equal estimations make it less slanted to be resolved to have malignancy.

Fatty Intake

The body needs calories for daily activities and looks after temperature, development, and sufficient body weight. Calories are provided mostly via starches and fats. The standard caloric necessity of CKD patients is 35 - 40 kcal/kg body weight every day. If caloric intake is insufficient, the body uses protein to get calories. This breakdown of protein can prompt severe impacts, for example, lack of healthy sustenance and a more prominent composition of waste items. It is necessary to give a sufficient measure of calories to CKD patients. It is essential to ascertain the caloric necessity indicated by a patient's optimal body weight and not current weight.

Starches

These are the essential source of calories for the body. Starches are found in wheat, grains, rice, potatoes, organic products, sugar, nectar, treats, cakes, desserts, and beverages. People with diabetes and fat patients need to confine the measure of starches. It is ideal to use complex sugars from grains like entire wheat and unpolished rice, giving fiber. These should form a large segment of the sugars in the eating regimen. All other essential sugar-containing substances should include not over 20% of the total starch consumption, particularly in diabetic patients. Non-diabetic patients may exchange calories from protein with starches as natural products, pies, cakes, treats, jam, or nectar as long as sweets with chocolate, nuts, or bananas are restricted.

Unsaturated or great fats like olive oil, nut oil, canola oil, safflower oil, sunflower oil, fish, and nuts are superior to saturated or terrible fats, for example, red meat, poultry, whole milk, margarine, ghee, cheese, coconut, and grease. Patients with CKD ought to diminish their intake of immersed fats and cholesterol, as these can cause heart disease. Excessive omega-6 polyunsaturated fats (PUFA) and a too-high omega-6/omega-3 proportion are unsafe, while low omega-6/omega-3 balance applies valuable impacts. Blends of vegetable oil, as opposed to single oil use, will accomplish this reason. Trans fat-containing substances like potato chips, doughnuts, financially arranged treats, and cakes are potentially hurtful and should be avoided.

Limit Protein Intake

Protein is fundamental for the fix and upkeep of body tissues. It additionally helps in the mending of wounds and battling against disease. Protein confinement (< 0.8 gm/kg body weight/day) is prescribed for CKD patients not on dialysis to diminish the pace of decreased kidney function and defer dialysis and kidney transplantation requirements. Serious protein restriction should be kept away from anyway, given the danger of lack of healthy sustenance. Low craving is normal in CKD patients. Poor hunger and severe protein restriction together can prompt poor nutrition, weight reduction, absence of vitality, and decreased body opposition, which increment the danger of death. The consumption of protein enhancements and medications, like creatine utilized for muscle advancement, is best kept away from except if affirmed by a physician or dietician. Protein intake should be expanded to 1.0 – 1.2 gm./kg body weight/day to supplant the proteins lost during the methodology when a patient is on dialysis.

Fluid Intake

The kidneys play an important role in keeping the amount of water in the body by expelling excess fluid as urine. In patients with CKD, as the kidney function exacerbates, the volume of urine generally reduces. Decreased urine yield prompts fluid maintenance in the body, causing puffiness of the face, growing of the legs and hands, and hypertension. The gathering of fluid in the lungs (a condition called pneumonic blockage or edema) causes shortness of breath and trouble in relaxing. If this isn't controlled, it tends to be hazardous. Leg growing (edema), ascites (aggregation of fluid in the stomach pit), the brevity of breath, and weight gain in a brief period are the pieces of information that suggest fluid over-burden.

CHAPTER 5:

Breakfast Recipes

1.   Mexican Scrambled Eggs in Tortilla

Preparation Time: 5 minutes

Cooking Time: 2 minutes

Servings: 2

Ingredients:

- 2 medium corn tortillas

- 4 egg whites

- 1 tsp. of cumin

- 3 tsp. of green chilies, diced

- 1/2 tsp. of hot pepper sauce

- 2 tbsp. of salsa

- 1/2 tsp. salt

Directions:

1. Spray some cooking spray on a medium skillet and heat for a few seconds.

2. Whisk the eggs with the green chilies, hot sauce, and cumin.

3. Add the eggs into the pan, and whisk with a spatula to scramble. Add the salt.

4. Cook until fluffy and done (1-2 minutes) over low heat.

5. Open the tortillas and spread 1 tbsp. of salsa on each.

6. Distribute the egg mixture onto the tortillas and wrap gently to make a burrito.

7. Serve warm.

Nutrition:

- Calories: 44.1

- Carbohydrate: 2.23 g

- Protein: 7.69 g

- Sodium: 854 mg

- Potassium: 189 mg

- Phosphorus: 22 mg

- Dietary Fiber: 0.5 g

- Fat: 0.39 g

2.   Egg White and Broccoli Omelet

Preparation Time: 5 minutes

Cooking Time: 4 minutes

Servings: 2

Ingredients:

- 4 egg whites

- 1/3 cup of boiled broccoli

- 1/2 tsp. of Dill

- 1 tbsp. of parmesan cheese, grated

- Salt/Pepper

Directions:

1. Put egg whites in a bowl. Mix until stiff and white.

2. Add the dill, the broccoli, and the parmesan cheese and incorporate everything with a spatula (do not over whisk).

3. Prepare the pan with a bit of cooking spray. Pour the egg and broccoli mixture. Cook around 1-2 minutes on each side.

4. Turn the omelet in half and optionally garnish with just a little bit of cheese on top.

Nutrition:

- Calories: 56.82 Carbohydrate: 2.7 g

- Protein: 10.57 g Sodium: 271.9 mg

- Potassium: 168.74 mg

- Phosphorus: 50.8 mg

- Dietary Fiber: 0.79 g Fat: 1.65 g

3.   Yogurt Parfait with Strawberries

Preparation Time: 3 minutes

Cooking Time: 1 minute

Servings: 2

Ingredients:

- 1/2 cup of soy yogurt (plain)

- 1 scoop of vanilla flavored protein

- 5 fresh strawberries, sliced

- 1 tbsp. of agave syrup

Directions:

1. In a bowl, slowly whisk the protein powder with the yogurt.

2. Add the strawberry slices and the agave syrup on top. Serve.

Nutrition:

- Calories: 153.25 Carbohydrate: 23.5 g Protein: 12.67 g Sodium: 93.32 mg Potassium: 85.9 mg Phosphorus: 62.75 mg Dietary Fiber: 1.43 g Fat: 1.17 g

4.   Raspberry Peach Breakfast Smoothie

Preparation Time: 3 minutes

Cooking Time: 1 minute

Servings: 2

Ingredients:

- 1/3 cup of raspberries, (it can be frozen)

- 1/2 peach, skin and pit removed

- 1 tbsp. of honey

- 1 cup of coconut water

Directions:

1. Prepare all ingredients in a blender and mix until smooth.

2. Pour and serve chilled in a tall glass or mason jar.

Nutrition:

- Calories: 86.3 Carbohydrate: 20.6 g Protein: 1.4 g Sodium: 3 mg Potassium: 109 mg Phosphorus: 36.08 mg Dietary Fiber: 2.6 g

- Fat: 0.31 g

5.   Mango Lassi Smoothie

Preparation Time: 5 minutes

Cooking Time: 1 minute

Servings: 2

Ingredients:

- 1/2 cup of plain yogurt

- 1/2 cup of plain water

- 1/2 cup of sliced mango

- 1 tbsp. of sugar

- 1/4 tsp. of cardamom

- 1/4 tsp. cinnamon

- 1/4 cup lime juice

Directions:

1. Pulse all the above ingredients in a blender until smooth (around 1 minute).

2. Pour into tall glasses or mason jars and serve chilled immediately.

Nutrition:

- Calories: 89.02

- Carbohydrate: 14.31 g

- Protein: 2.54 g

- Sodium: 30 mg

- Potassium: 185.67 mg

- Phosphorus: 67.88 mg

- Dietary Fiber: 0.77 g

- Fat: 2.05 g

CHAPTER 6:

Lunch Recipes

6.   Baked Pork Chops

Preparation Time:

Cooking time: 40 minutes

Servings: 6

Ingredients:

- 1/2 cup flour

- 1 large egg

- 1/4 cup water

- 3/4 cup breadcrumbs

- 6 (3 1/2 oz.) pork chops

- 2 tablespoons butter, unsalted

- 1 teaspoon paprika

Directions:

1. Begin by switching the oven to 350 degrees F to preheat.

2. Mix and spread the flour on a shallow plate.

3. Whisk the egg with water in another shallow bowl.

4. Spread the breadcrumbs on a separate plate.

5. Firstly, coat the pork with flour, then dip in the egg mix and then in the crumbs.

6. Grease a baking sheet and place the chops on it.

7. Drizzle the pepper on top and bake for 40 minutes. Serve.

Nutrition:

- Calories 221 Fat 7.8g

- Cholesterol 93mg

- Carbohydrate 11.9g

- Sodium 135mg

- Phosphorous 299mg

- Potassium 391mg

- Dietary Fiber 3.5g

- Protein 24.7g

- Calcium 13mg

7.   Lasagna Rolls In Marinara Sauce

Preparation Time: 15 minutes

Cooking Time: 30 minutes

Servings: 9

Ingredients:

- 1/4 tsp. crushed red pepper

- 1/4 tsp. salt

- 1/2 cup shredded mozzarella cheese

- 1/2 cups parmesan cheese, shredded

- 1 14-oz package tofu, cubed

- 1 25-oz of low-sodium marinara sauce

- 1 tbsp. extra virgin olive oil

- 12 whole wheat lasagna noodles

- 2 tbsp. Kalamata olives, chopped

- 3 cloves minced garlic

- 3 cups spinach, chopped

Directions:

1. Put enough water on a large pot and cook the lasagna noodles according to package direction.

2. In a large skillet, sauté garlic over medium heat for 20 seconds. Add the tofu and spinach and cook until the spinach wilts.

3. Move mixture to a bowl and add parmesan olives, salt, red pepper, and 2/3 cup of the marinara sauce.

4. In a pan, spread a cup of marinara sauce on the bottom. To make the rolls, place noodles on a surface and spread 1/4 cup of the tofu filling.

5. Roll up and place it on the pan with the marinara sauce. Do this procedure until all lasagna noodles are rolled.

6. Place the pan and bring to a simmer. Reduce the heat to medium and let it cook for three more minutes.

7. Sprinkle mozzarella cheese and let the cheese melt for two minutes. Serve hot.

Nutrition:

- Calories: 600 Carbs: 65g

- Protein: 36g Fats: 26g;

- Sodium: 1194mg Potassium: 914mg

- Phosphorus: 627mg

8.   Steak with Onion

Preparation Time: 5 minutes

Cooking Time: 1 hour

Servings: 7 – 8

Ingredients:

- 1/4 Cup of white flour

- 1/8 Teaspoon of ground black pepper

- 1 and ½ pounds of round steak of ¾ inch of thickness each

- 2 Tablespoons of oil

- 1 Cup of water

- 1 tablespoon of vinegar

- 1 Minced garlic clove

- 1 to 2 bay leaves

- 1/4 teaspoon of crushed dried thyme

- 3 Sliced medium onions

Directions:

1. Cut the steak into about 7 to 8 equal servings. Combine the flour and the pepper, then pound the ingredients all together into the meat.

2. Cook the meat on both its sides.

3. Get the meat from the skillet and set it aside.

4. Combine the water with the vinegar, the garlic, the bay leaf, and the thyme in the skillet; then bring the mixture to a boil.

5. Place the meat in the mixture and cover it with onion slices.

6. Cover your ingredients and let simmer for about 55 to 60 minutes

7. Serve and enjoy your lunch!

Nutrition:

- Calories: 286

- Fats: 18g

- Carbs: 12g

- Fiber: 2.25g

- Sodium: 45mg

- Potassium: 368mg

- Phosphorous: 180mg

- Protein 19g

9.   Chicken Paella

Preparation Time: 5 minutes

Cooking Time: 10 minutes

Servings: 8

Ingredients:

- ½ Pound of skinned, boned, and cut into pieces chicken breasts

- 1/4 Cup of water

- 1 Can of 10-1/2 oz. of low-sodium chicken broth

- 1/2 Pound of peeled and cleaned medium-size shrimp

- 1/2 Cup of frozen green pepper

- 1/3 cup of chopped red bell

- 1/3 cup of thinly sliced green onion

- 2 Minced garlic cloves

- 1/4 Teaspoon of pepper

- 1 Dash of ground saffron

- 1 Cup of uncooked instant white rice

Directions:

1. Prepare and combine the first 3 ingredients in a medium casserole, cover it with a lid, then microwave it for about 4 minutes.

2. Stir in the shrimp and the following 6 ingredients; then cover and microwave the shrimp on high heat for about 3 and 1/2 minutes

3. Stir in the rice; then cover and set aside for about 5 minutes

4. Serve and enjoy your paella.

Nutrition:

- Calories: 236

- Fats: 11g

- Carbs: 6g

- Fiber: 1.2g

- Sodium: 83mg

- Potassium: 178mg

- Phosphorous: 144mg

- Protein 28g

10. Beef Kabobs with Pepper

Preparation Time: 5 minutes

Cooking Time: 10 minutes

Servings: 8

Ingredients:

- 1 Pound of beef sirloin

- ½ Cup of vinegar

- 2 tbsp. of salad oil

- 1 medium chopped onion

- 2 tbsp. of chopped fresh parsley

- 1/4 tsp. of black pepper

- 2 Cut into strips green peppers

Directions:

1. Trim the fat from the meat. Cut it into cubes of 1 and 1/2 inches each.

2. Mix the vinegar, the oil, the onion, the parsley, and the pepper in a bowl

3. Place the meat in the marinade and set it aside for about 2 hours; make sure to stir from time to time.

4. Prepare it by alternating on skewers instead with green pepper.

5. Brush the pepper with the marinade and broil for about 10 minutes 4 inches from the heat

6. Serve and enjoy your kabobs.

Nutrition:

- Calories: 357

- Fats: 24g

- Carbs: 9g

- Fiber: 2.3g

- Sodium: 60mg

- Potassium: 250mg

- Phosphorous: 217mg

- Protein 26g

CHAPTER 7:

Dinner Recipes

11.   Chicken Casserole

Preparation Time: 15 minutes Cooking Time: 45 minutes

Servings: 6

Ingredients:

- 1/4 cup jalapeno pepper slices (optional)

- 1 cup shredded reduced-fat Monterey Jack cheese

- 4 garlic cloves (crushed)

- 1 tbsp. cumin

- 1 tbsp. chili powder

- 1 cup chopped Poblano pepper

- 1 cup chopped red bell pepper

- 1 cup frozen yellow corn kernels

- 1 (15 ounces) can black beans (no salt added, drained, and rinsed)

- 2 (14.5 ounces) cans tomatoes (no salt added, diced or crushed)

- 1-pound skinless, boneless chicken breast, and cut into bite-sized pieces

- 1 1/2 cups cooked rice (preferably brown)

Directions:

1. Ensure to preheat the oven first to 400oF.

2. In a bowl, combine garlic, peppers, seasonings, beans, corns, and tomatoes.

3. Then, in a shallow 3-quart casserole, spread the rice topped with chicken.

4. Pour over chicken casserole the mixed ingredients and bake for around 45 minutes. Serve.

Nutrition:

- Calories: 393 Carbs: 39g

- Protein: 39g Fats: 9g

- Sodium: 433mg

- Potassium: 824mg

- Phosphorus: 457mg

12.   Vegetable Lovers Chicken Soup

Preparation Time: 10 minutes

Cooking Time: 20 minutes

Servings: 6

Ingredients:

- 1 1/2 cups baby spinach

- 2 tbsp. orzo (tiny pasta)

- 1 tbsp. dry white wine

- 1 14oz low sodium chicken broth

- 2 plum tomatoes, chopped

- ½ tsp. Italian seasoning

- 1 large shallot, chopped

- 1 small zucchini, diced

- 8oz chicken tenders

- 1 tbsp. extra virgin olive oil

Directions:

1. Get a large saucepan and heat oil over medium heat. Add the chicken. Stir occasionally for four minutes until browned. Transfer on a plate. Set aside.

2. In the same saucepan, add the zucchini, Italian seasoning, shallot, and salt and often stir until the vegetables are softened.

3. Add the tomatoes, wine, broth, and orzo and increase the heat to high to bring the mixture to boil. Simmer for 3 minutes on low heat.

4. Add the cooked chicken and stir in the spinach last. Serve hot.

Nutrition:

- Calories: 80

- Carbs: 5g

- Protein: 10g

- Fats: 3g

- Sodium: 75mg

- Potassium: 258mg

- Phosphorus: 112mg

13. Herbed Soup with Black Beans

Preparation Time: 10 minutes

Cooking Time: 10 minutes

Servings: 4

Ingredients:

- 2 tbsps. tomato paste

- 1/3 cup Poblano pepper, charred, peeled, seeded, and chopped

- 2 cups vegetable stock

- 1/4 tsp. cumin

- 1/2 tsp. paprika

- 1/2 tsp. dried oregano

- 2 tsp. fresh garlic, minced

- 1 cup onion, small diced

- 1 tbsp. extra-virgin olive oil

- 1 15 oz. can black beans

Directions:

1. On medium fire, place a soup pot and heat oil.

2. Sauté onion until translucent and soft, around 4-5 minutes.

3. Add garlic, cook for 2 minutes.

4. Add the rest of the ingredients and bring to a simmer. Once simmering, turn off the fire and transfer to a blender.

5. Puree ingredients until smooth.

6. You can serve right away or serve cold.

7. Soup can also be stored in the refrigerator for up to 3 days.

Nutrition:

- Calories: 100

- Carbs: 16g

- Protein: 4g

- Fats: 3g

- Sodium: 322mg

- Potassium: 451mg

- Phosphorus: 79mg

14.   Creamy Pumpkin Soup

Preparation Time: 10 minutes

Cooking Time: 20 minutes

Servings: 4

Ingredients:

- 1 onion, chopped

- 1 slice of bacon

- 2 tsp. ground ginger

- 1 tsp. cinnamon

- 1 cup applesauce

- 3 1/2 cups low sodium chicken broth

- 1 29-oz can pumpkin

- Pepper to taste

- 1/2 cup light sour cream

Directions:

1. On medium-high fire, place a soup pot and add bacon once hot. Sauté until crispy, around 5 minutes.

2. Discard bacon fat before continuing to cook.

3. Add ginger, applesauce, chicken broth, and pumpkin. Season lightly with pepper.

4. Let it simmer and cook for 10 minutes.

5. Taste and adjust seasoning.

6. Turn off fire, stir in sour cream, and mix well.

7. Serve and enjoy while hot.

Nutrition:

- Calories: 224

- Carbs: 34g

- Protein: 8g

- Fats: 8g

- Sodium: 132mg

- Potassium: 855mg

- Phosphorus: 188mg

15.   Broccoli, Arugula, and Avocado Cream Soup

Preparation Time: 10 minutes

Cooking Time: 10 minutes

Servings: 2

Ingredients:

- 1/4 tsp. red pepper flakes

- 1/2 Haas avocado

- 1 cup of water

- 1 tbsp. apple cider vinegar

- 1 tbsp. honey

- 1 tbsp. olive oil

- 1/3 medium onion

- 1-inch minced ginger root

- 2 handfuls arugula

- 8-10 decent sized broccoli clusters

- Juice from half a lemon

Directions:

1. Steam broccoli for at least 5-7 minutes or until bright green.

2. In a saucepan, on medium-high fire and heat oil. Add onions and sauté until translucent.

3. In a blender, add all ingredients, including cooked onion and broccoli, plus a half cup of water.

4. Blend until smooth and creamy.

5. You can serve hot or cold.

Nutrition:

- Calories: 206

- Carbs: 20g

- Protein: 3g

- Fats: 14g

- Sodium: 25mg

- Potassium: 529mg

- Phosphorus: 75mg

CHAPTER 8:

Soup Recipes

16.   Curried Carrot and Beet Soup

Preparation Time: 10 minutes

Cooking Time: 50 minutes

Servings: 4

Ingredients:

- 1 large red beet

- 5 carrots, chopped

- 1 tablespoon curry powder

- 3 cups Homemade Rice Milk or unsweetened store-bought rice milk

- Freshly ground black pepper

- Yogurt, for serving

Directions:

1. Preheat the oven to 400°F.

2. Cover beet in aluminum foil and roast for 45 minutes, until the vegetable is tender when pierced with a fork. Remove from the oven and let cool.

3. Prepare the carrots in a saucepan and cover with water. Bring to a boil and simmer for 10 minutes until tender.

4. Transfer the carrots and beet to a food processor and process until smooth.

5. Add the curry powder and rice milk. Season it with pepper. Serve topped with a dollop of yogurt.

Nutrition:

- Calories: 186

- Fat: 11g

- Carbohydrates: 17g

- Protein: 7g

- Sodium: 248mg

- Potassium: 357mg

- Phosphorus: 225mg

17.   Asparagus Lemon Soup

Preparation Time: 10 minutes

Cooking Time: 25 minutes

Servings: 4

Ingredients:

- 1-pound asparagus

- 2 tablespoons extra-virgin olive oil

- ½ sweet onion, chopped

- 4 cups low-sodium chicken stock

- ½ cup Homemade Rice Milk or unsweetened store-bought rice milk

- Freshly ground black pepper

- Juice of 1 lemon

Directions:

1. Cut the asparagus tips from the spears and set aside.

2. Heat the olive oil in a small stockpot. Add the onion and cook, frequently stirring for 3 to 5 minutes, until it softens.

3. Add the stock and asparagus stalks and bring to a boil. Simmer until the asparagus is tender.

4. Put to a blender or food processor and carefully purée until smooth. Return to the pot, add the asparagus tips, and simmer until tender, about 5 minutes.

5. Add the rice milk, pepper, and lemon juice, and stir until heated through. Serve.

Nutrition:

- Calories: 86

- Fat: 11g

- Carbohydrates: 17g

- Protein: 7g

- Sodium: 128mg

- Potassium: 257mg

- Phosphorus: 155mg

18. Cauliflower and Chive Soup

Preparation Time: 10 minutes

Cooking Time: 20 minutes

Servings: 4

Ingredients:

- 2 tablespoons extra-virgin olive oil

- ½ sweet onion, chopped

- 2 garlic cloves, minced

- 2 cups Simple Chicken Broth or low-sodium store-bought chicken stock

- 1 cauliflower head, broken into florets

- Freshly ground black pepper

- 4 tablespoons (¼ cups) finely chopped chives

Directions:

1. Heat the olive oil. Add and cook the onion, frequently stirring, until it softens for 3 to 5 minutes.

2. Add the garlic and stir until fragrant.

3. Add the broth and cauliflower and bring to a boil. Reduce the heat and simmer until the cauliflower is tender, about 15 minutes.

4. Put the soup in a blender or processor and purée until smooth.

5. Return the soup to the pot, and season with pepper. Before serving, top each bowl with 1 tablespoon of chives.

Nutrition:

- Calories: 156 Fat: 11g

- Carbohydrates: 17g Protein: 7g

- Sodium: 248mg Potassium: 527mg

- Phosphorus: 125mg

19.   Simple Chicken and Rice Soup

Preparation Time: 10 minutes

Cooking Time: 15 minutes

Servings: 4

Ingredients:

- 1 tablespoon extra-virgin olive oil

- ½ sweet onion, chopped

- 2 celery stalks, chopped

- 2 carrots, chopped

- 8 ounces chicken breast, diced

- 4 cups Simple Chicken Broth or low-sodium store-bought chicken stock

- ¼ teaspoon dried thyme leaves

- 1 cup cooked rice

- Juice of 1 lime

- Freshly ground black pepper

- 2 tablespoons chopped parsley leaves for garnish

Directions:

1. Heat the olive oil over medium-high heat. Add the onion, celery, carrots, and cook, often stirring, for about 5 minutes, until the onion begins to soften.

2. Add the chicken breast and continue stirring until the meat is just browned but not cooked through. Add the broth and thyme and bring to a boil.

3. Simmer for 10 minutes, until the chicken is cooked through and the vegetables are tender.

4. Add the rice and lime juice. Season it with pepper. Serve and garnished with parsley leaves.

Nutrition:

- Calories: 176

- Fat: 11g

- Carbohydrates: 17g

- Protein: 7g

- Sodium: 128mg

- Potassium: 357mg

- Phosphorus: 225mg

20.   Turkey, Wild Rice, and Mushroom Soup

Preparation Time: 15 minutes

Cooking Time: 2-3 hours

Servings: 6

Ingredients:

- ½ cup onion, chopped

- ½ cup red bell pepper, chopped

- ½ cup carrots, chopped

- 2 garlic cloves, minced

- 2 cup cooked turkey, shredded

- 5 cup chicken broth (see recipe)

- ½ cup quick-cooking wild rice, uncooked

- 1 tbsp. olive oil

- 1 cup mushrooms, sliced

- 2 bay leaves

- ¼ tsp. Mrs. Dash® Original salt-free herb seasoning blend

- 1 tsp. dried thyme

- ½ tsp. low sodium salt

- ¼ tsp. black pepper

Directions:

1. Cook rice in a saucepan with 1-2 cups of broth. Set aside.

2. Heat the oil in a skillet and sauté the onion, bell pepper, carrots, and garlic until soft.

3. Add other ingredients to the slow cooker except for the rice and mushrooms.

4. Cook for 2-3 hours on low with cover.

5. Put the mushrooms and rice. Cook for another 15 minutes.

6. Remove the bay leaves and serve.

Nutrition:

- Calories: 136 Fat: 11g

- Carbohydrates: 15g Protein: 5g

- Sodium: 128mg Potassium: 537mg

- Phosphorus: 145mg

CHAPTER 9:

Fish and Seafood Recipes

21.   Shrimp in Garlic Sauce

Preparation Time: 10 minutes

Cooking Time: 3 minutes

Servings: 4

Ingredients:

- 1/2 lb. raw shrimp, shelled & deveined

- 8 oz. bowtie pasta, cooked

- 3 tablespoons unsalted butter

- 3 garlic cloves

- 1/4 cup onion

- 1/2 cup whipped cream cheese

- 1/4 cup half & half cream

- 1/4 cup white wine

- 2 tablespoons fresh basil

- 1/8 teaspoon black pepper

Directions:

1. Start by melting the butter in the Instant Pot on sauté mode.

2. Add onion and garlic to sauté for 1 minute.

3. Toss in the remaining ingredients to the insert.

4. Seal the lid and cook for 2 minutes on Manual mode at High pressure.

5. Serve warm with cooked pasta.

Nutrition:

- Calories 336

- Fats 13g

- Carbs 31.5g

- Fiber 1.3g

- Protein 21g

- Sodium: 636mg

- Potassium: 137.5mg

- Phosphorus: 104mg

22. Eggplant Seafood Casserole

Preparation Time: 10 minutes

Cooking Time: 20 minutes

Servings: 4

Ingredients:

- 2 medium eggplant, diced

- 1 medium onion, diced

- 1 bell pepper, diced

- 1/2 cup celery, chopped

- 2 garlic cloves, minced

- 1/4 cup olive oil

- 1/4 cup lemon juice

- 1 tablespoon Worcestershire sauce

- 1/4 teaspoons salt-free Creole seasoning

- 1/2 teaspoons hot pepper sauce

- 1/3 cup rice, uncooked

- 1/4 cup Parmesan cheese

- 1 dash cayenne pepper

- 3 eggs

- 1 lb. lump crab meat

- 1/2 lb. boiled shrimp

- 1/2 cup breadcrumbs

- 2 tablespoons unsalted butter, melted

Directions:

1. Boil eggplant with water in a saucepan for 5 minutes.

2. Drain the eggplant and keep it aside.

3. Now sauté the onion with celery, bell pepper, garlic, and oil in the Instant Pot on Sauté mode.

4. Transfer these veggies to the eggplant along with all other ingredients except the breadcrumbs.

5. Mix well, then spread this mixture into a casserole dish suitable to fit in the Instant Pot.

6. Pour 1.5 cup water into the Instant pot and place a trivet over it.

7. Set the casserole dish over the trivet. Spread the crumbs over the casserole.

8. Seal the lid and cook for 15 minutes on Manual mode at High pressure.

9. Remove the pot's lid when done. Serve warm.

Nutrition:

- Calories 216

- Fats 12 g

- Carbs 14 g

- Fiber 2.3 g

- Protein 13 g

- Sodium: 482mg

- Potassium: 690mg

- Phosphorus: 182mg

23.   Halibut with Lemon Caper Sauce

Preparation Time: 10 minutes

Cooking Time: 10 minutes

Servings: 4

Ingredients:

- 4 tablespoons lemon juice

- 1 tablespoon olive oil

- 20 oz. raw halibut steaks

- 2 tablespoons unsalted butter

- 2 teaspoons almond flour

- 1/2 cup reduced-sodium chicken broth

- 1/4 cup white wine

- 1 teaspoon capers

- 1/4 teaspoons white pepper

Directions:

1. Season the halibut steaks with 2 tablespoons of lemon juice and olive oil in a bowl.

2. Now melt butter in the instant pot on Sauté mode.

3. Stir in the remaining ingredients and whisk well.

4. Place a steamer basket over the sauce mixture and add halibut to the basket.

5. Seal the lid and cook for 5 minutes on Manual mode at High pressure.

6. Once done, release the pressure completely, then remove the pot's lid.

7. Remove the fish and the basket.

8. Add the fish to the sauce and mix well gently. Serve warm.

Nutrition:

- Calories 260 Fats 10g

- Carbs 5g Protein 36g

- Sodium 118 mg Potassium: 573mg

- Phosphorus: 306mg

CHAPTER 10:

Poultry and Meat Recipes

24.   Lemon & Herb Chicken Wraps

Preparation Time: 5 minutes

Cooking Time: 30 minutes

Servings: 4

Ingredients:

- 4 oz. skinless and sliced chicken breasts

- 1/2 sliced red bell pepper

- 1 lemon

- 4 large iceberg lettuce leaves

- 1 tbsp. olive oil

- 2 tbsps. Finely chopped fresh cilantro

- 1/4 tsp. black pepper

Directions:

1. Preheat the oven to 375°F.

2. Mix the oil, juice of ½ lemon, cilantro, and black pepper.

3. Marinate the chicken in the oil marinade, cover, and leave in the fridge for as long as possible.

4. Wrap the chicken in parchment paper, drizzling over the remaining marinade.

5. Place in the oven in an oven dish for 25-30 minutes or until chicken is thoroughly cooked through and white inside.

6. Divide the sliced bell pepper and layer it onto each lettuce leaf.

7. Divide the chicken onto each lettuce leaf and squeeze over the remaining lemon juice to taste. Wrap and enjoy.

Nutrition:

- Calories 364

- Protein 35g

- Carbs 32g

- Fat 10g

- Sodium 398mg

- Potassium 413mg

- Phosphorus 264mg

25. Chinese Beef Wraps

Preparation Time: 10 minutes

Cooking Time: 30 minutes

Servings: 2

Ingredients:

- 2 iceberg lettuce leaves

- 1/2 diced cucumber

- 1 tsp. canola oil

- 5 oz. lean ground beef

- 1 tsp. ground ginger

- 1 tbsp. chili flakes

- 1 minced garlic clove

- 1 tbsp. rice wine vinegar

Directions:

1. Mix the ground meat with garlic, rice wine vinegar, chili flakes, and ginger in a bowl.

2. Get a skillet and heat over medium flame.

3. Add the beef to the pan and cook for 20-25 minutes or until cooked through.

4. Serve beef mixture with diced cucumber in each lettuce wrap and fold.

Nutrition:

- Calories 205

- Fat 12g

- Carbs 16g

- Protein 8.7g

- Sodium 347mg

- Phosphorus 101mg

- Potassium 408mg

CHAPTER 11:

Smoothies Recipes

26.   Carrot and Pineapple Slaw

Preparation Time: 5 minutes

Cooking Time: 5 minutes

Servings: 2

Ingredients:

- 5 ounces Carrot matchsticks

- 1/2 cup Pineapple chunks, canned, liquid drained

- 1/2 cup Grapes, sliced in half

- 1/4 cup Pecan pieces

- 1/8 cup Mayonnaise, low sodium

- 1 tablespoon Lemon juice

Directions:

1. In a bowl, toss together the carrot matchsticks, drained pineapple chunks, sliced grapes, and pecan pieces.

2. Stir in the low-sodium mayonnaise and lemon juice.

3. Cover the bowl and then allow it to chill and marinate for at least an hour before serving. You can make this slaw up to a day in advance.

Nutrition:

- Calories: 215 Fat: 15g

- Sodium: 136mg

- Potassium: 353mg

- Phosphorus: 74mg

- Carbs: 20g Protein: 3g

27.   Sesame Cucumber Salad

Preparation Time: 5 minutes

Cooking Time: 5 minutes

Servings: 2

Ingredients:

- 1 Cucumbers, thinly sliced

- 1/2 teaspoon Sesame seeds

- 1 tablespoon Rice wine vinegar

- 1/2 tablespoon Sugar

- 1 1/2 tablespoons Sesame seed oil

- 1/4 teaspoon Red pepper flakes

Directions:

1. You want the cucumbers sliced as thinly as you can get them. While you can certainly do this with a knife, it is quicker and easier to use a mandolin.

2. In a medium to a small bowl, whisk together the sesame seeds, rice wine vinegar, sugar, sesame seed oil, and red pepper flakes.

3. Once well combined, add in the cucumbers and toss the vegetables in the vinaigrette.

4. Serve immediately.

Nutrition:

- Calories: 92

- Fat: 5g

- Sodium: 117mg

- Potassium: 250mg

- Phosphorus: 46mg

- Carbs: 7.6g

- Protein: 1.87g

28.   Creamy Jalapeno Corn

Preparation Time: 5 minutes

Cooking Time: 15 minutes

Servings: 2

Ingredients:

- 1 cup Corn kernels, fresh

- 1/4 cup Red bell pepper, diced

- 1 Jalapeno, seeded and diced

- 1/2 ounces Cream cheese

- 1 tablespoon Olive oil

- 1/4 teaspoon Black pepper, ground

- 1/4 cup Cheddar cheese, low sodium

Directions:

1. Preheat your oven to a Fahrenheit temperature of three-hundred and fifty degrees.

2. In a medium saucepan, sauté the bell pepper and jalapeno in the olive oil until softened, about four minutes.

3. Put cream cheese and continue to stir until it melts and combines with the vegetables.

4. Add in the corn, black pepper, and half of the cheese. After the mixture is combined, sprinkle the remaining cheese over the top.

5. Put the saucepan in the oven to cook until it is hot and bubbling for fifteen minutes.

Nutrition:

- Calories: 284

- Fat: 19g

- Sodium: 82mg

- Potassium: 293mg

- Phosphorus: 200mg

- Carbs: 20g

- Protein: 7g

29. Hazelnut Cinnamon Coffee

Preparation Time: 5 minutes

Cooking Time: 2 minutes

Servings: 1

Ingredients:

- 1 1/2 cups fresh brewed Toasted Hazelnut Blend

- 1 cup half & half

- 1/4 cup chocolate syrup

- 2 tablespoons hazelnut syrup

- 1/8 teaspoon ground cinnamon

Directions:

1. Add hot coffee to a 1-quart saucepan.

2. Steadily add all remaining ingredients, then stir.

3. Cook at medium temperature.

4. Put a sprinkle of cinnamon on top and enjoy.

Nutrition:

- Calories: 161

- Fat: 7g

- Carbs: 23g

- Protein: 2g

- Sodium: 34.6mg

- Potassium: 219mg

- Phosphorus: 100mg

30.   Pina Colada Protein Smoothie

Preparation Time: 5 minutes Cooking Time: 2 minutes

Servings: 1

Ingredients:

- 1/2 cup unsweetened vanilla almond milk

- 1/2 cup unsweetened coconut milk

- 3/4 cup frozen pineapple chunks

- 1 scoop vanilla protein powder

- 1 tsp. raw honey

- 1 tsp. vanilla

Directions:

1. Place almond milk, coconut milk, pineapple, vanilla protein powder, honey, and vanilla in a blender.

2. Blend until smooth. Serve immediately.

Nutrition:

- Calories: 241 Fat: 7g Carbs: 20g Protein: 26g

- Sodium: 420mg Potassium: 205mg Phosphorus: 10mg

CHAPTER 12:

Snack Recipes

31. Mixes of Snacks

Preparation Time: 15 minutes

Cooking Time: 1 hour

Servings: 1

Ingredients:

- 6 c. margarine
- 2 tbsp. Worcestershire sauce
- 1 ½ tbsp. spice salt
- ¾ c. garlic powder
- ½ tsp. onion powder

- 3 cups Cheerios

- 3 cups corn flakes - 1 cup pretzel

- 1 cup broken bagel chip into 1-inch pieces

Directions:

1. Preheat the oven to 250F (120C)

2. Melt the margarine in a large roasting pan. Stir in the seasoning. Gradually add the remaining ingredients by mixing so that the coating is uniform.

3. Cook 1 hour, stirring every 15 minutes.

4. Spread on paper towels to let cool. Store in a tightly closed container.

Nutrition:

- Calories: 150 Fat: 6g

- Carbs: 20g Protein: 3g

- Sodium: 300mg Potassium: 93mg

- Phosphorus: 70mg

32. Spicy Crab Dip

Preparation Time: 10 minutes

Cooking Time: 20 minutes

Servings: 1

Ingredients:

- 1 can of 8 oz. softened cream cheese

- 1 tbsp. finely chopped onions

- 1 tbsp. lemon juice

- 2 tbsp. Worcestershire sauce

- 1/8 tsp. black pepper Cayenne pepper to taste

- 2 tbsp. of milk or non-fortified rice drink

- 1 can of 6 oz. of crabmeat

Directions:

1. Preheat the oven to 375 degrees F.

2. Pour the cheese cream into a bowl. Add the onions, lemon juice, Worcestershire sauce, black pepper, and cayenne pepper. Mix well. Stir in the milk/rice drink.

3. Add the crabmeat and mix until you obtain a homogeneous mixture.

4. Pour the mixture into a baking dish. Cook without covering for 15 minutes or until bubbles appear. Serve hot with low-sodium crackers or triangle cut pita bread.

5. Microwave until bubbles appear, about 4 minutes, stirring every 1 to 2 minutes.

Nutrition:

- Calories: 42

- Fat: 0.5g

- Carbs: 2g

- Protein: 7g

- Sodium: 167mg

- Potassium: 130mg

- Phosphorus: 139mg

33. Sesame Crackers

Preparation Time: 15 minutes

Cooking Time: 12 minutes

Servings: 1

Ingredients:

- 1 cup sesame seeds

- 2 tbsp. grapeseed oil

- 2 large eggs, beaten

- 1 ½ tsp. sea salt

- 3 cups almond flour

Directions:

1. Mix well the sesame seeds, almond flour, oil, eggs, and salt in a bowl.

2. Place each into two baking sheets and cover with parchment paper.

3. Lay the dough between the papers to cover the entire baking sheet and remove the top paper.

4. Cut dough into 2-inch squares and bake at 350°F until golden brown, for about 12 minutes.

5. Cool before serving.

Nutrition:

- Calories: 178 Fat: 15.6 g

- Carbs: 6 g

- Protein: 6.1 g

- Sodium: 184 mg

- Potassium: 468mg

- Phosphorus: 0mg

34.   Veggie Snack

Preparation Time: 5 minutes

Cooking Time: 10 minutes

Servings: 1

Ingredients:

- 1 large yellow pepper

- 5 carrots

- 5 stalks celery

Directions:

1. Clean the carrots and rinse under running water.

2. Rinse celery and yellow pepper. Remove seeds of pepper and chop the veggies into small sticks.

3. Put in a bowl and serve.

Nutrition:

- Calories: 189 Fat: 0.5 g Carbs: 44.3 g Protein: 5 g

- Sodium: 282 mg Potassium: 0mg Phosphorus: 0mg

35. Healthy Spiced Nuts

Preparation Time: 10 minutes

Cooking Time: 10 minutes

Servings: 4

Ingredients:

- 1 tbsp. extra virgin olive oil

- ¼ cup walnuts

- ¼ cup pecans

- ¼ cup almonds

- ½ tsp. sea salt

- ½ tsp. cumin

- ½ tsp. pepper

- 1 tsp. chili powder

Directions:

1. Put the skillet on medium heat and toast the nuts until lightly browned.

2. Prepare the spice mixture and add black pepper, cumin, chili, and salt.

3. Put extra virgin olive oil and sprinkle with spice mixture to the toasted nuts before serving.

Nutrition:

- Calories: 88 Fat: 8g

- Carbs: 4g Protein: 2.5g

- Sodium: 51mg

- Potassium: 88mg

- Phosphorus: 6.3mg

CHAPTER 13:

Desserts Recipes

36.   Lemon Bars

Preparation Time: 20 minutes

Cooking Time: 45 minutes

Servings: 24

Ingredients:

For Crust

- 2 cups all-purpose flour

- 1 cup unsalted butter

- ½ cup powdered sugar or sugar replacement

For Filling

- ¼ cup all-purpose flour

- ¼ tsp. baking soda

- ½ tsp. cream of tartar

- 4 eggs

- 1 ½ cups sugar or sugar replacement

- ¼ cup lemon juice

For Glaze

- 2 tbsp. lemon juice

- 1 cup sifted powdered sugar or sugar replacement

Directions:

For Crust

1. Preheat oven to 350° F. Mix flour, powdered sugar, and butter in a large bowl until crumbly.

2. Press mixture into a 9-inch x 13-inch baking pan.

3. Bake for about 20 minutes until lightly browned.

For Filling

1. Gently whisk eggs in a medium-sized bowl.

2. Mix flour, sugar, soda, and cream of tartar in a separate bowl and add these ingredients to the eggs. Whisk lemon juice into the egg mixture until slightly thickened.

3. Pour over the warm crust and bake for another 20 minutes or until filling is set. Remove from the oven and allow to cool.

For Glaze

1. Slowly add the lemon juice into the sifted powdered sugar until spreadable.

2. Spread over cooled filling. Allow to set and then cut into 24 bars—store leftovers in the refrigerator.

Nutrition:

- Calories 200

- Protein 2 g

- Carbohydrates 28 g

- Sodium 27 mg

- Phosphorus 32 mg

- Potassium 41 mg

37.   Baked Pineapple

Preparation Time: 10 minutes

Cooking Time: 40 minutes

Servings: 1

Ingredients:

- 20 oz. canned, crushed pineapple with juice

- 2 large eggs or egg substitute

- 2 cups sugar or sugar replacement

- 3 tbsp. tapioca

- 1/2 tsp. cinnamon

- 1/8 tsp. salt

- 3 tbsp. unsalted butter

Directions:

1. Preheat oven to 350°F.

2. Put the crushed pineapple with juice into a bowl.

3. Beat two eggs and add to the crushed pineapple.

4. Put sugar, tapioca, and salt in the pineapple egg mixture.

5. Pour mixture into 8-inch square baking dish.

6. Cut butter and place on top of pineapple mixture and sprinkle with cinnamon—Bake for 30 minutes.

Nutrition:

- Calories 270 Carbohydrates 54 g

- Protein 2 g Sodium 50 mg

- Phosphorus 26 mg Potassium 85 mg

38.   Kidney-Friendly Vanilla Ice Cream

Preparation Time: 15 minutes

Cooking Time: 1 hour

Servings: 1

Ingredients:

- 1 cup low-cholesterol egg product

- ½ cup of sugar

- 2 cups liquid non-dairy creamer

- 1 tbsp. vanilla extract

- Rock salt

- Ice

Directions:

1. Beat egg and sugar in a large microwaveable bowl.

2. Stir in non-dairy creamer and microwave for one minute, or until mixture thickens. When cool, stir in vanilla.

3. Add the mixture into the center container of the ice cream machine and layer ice and rock salt around a container, alternating layers until the bucket is full.

4. Process according to the manufacturer's instructions for your particular ice cream machine.

Nutrition:

- Calories 159

- Carbohydrates 22 g

- Protein 3 g

- Sodium 64 mg

- Phosphorus 36 mg

- Potassium 87 mg

39.   Quick Cupcakes

Preparation Time: 10 minutes

Cooking Time: 10 minutes

Servings: 12

Ingredients:

- 1 box angel food cake mix

- 1 box lemon cake mix

- 2 tsp. water

- Non-stick cooking spray

Directions:

1. In a large zip-lock bag, pour in angel food cake mix and lemon cake mix. Seal the plastic bag and shake to mix together.

2. Spray non-stick cooking in a small custard dish and add three tablespoons of dry cake mix to the dish. Add two tablespoons of water and mix with a fork.

3. Microwave on high for one minute. Slip the muffin out of the dish and allow it to cool.

4. Repeat this process for as many cupcakes as you require.

Nutrition:

- Calories 97

- Carbohydrates 21 g

- Protein 1 g

- Sodium 163 mg

- Potassium 17 mg

- Phosphorus 80 mg

40. Peppermint Crunch Cookies

Preparation Time: 10 minutes

Cooking Time: 30 minutes

Servings: 18

Ingredients:

- 18 peppermint candies

- ¼ tsp. peppermint extract

- 1 ½ cups all-purpose flour

- 1 tsp. baking powder

- ¼ tsp. salt

- ¾ cup sugar or sugar replacement

- ½ cup soft unsalted butter

- 1 large egg or egg substitute

Directions:

1. Put the 12 peppermint candies in a zip-lock bag and pound with a heavy pan until finely crushed.

2. Add sugar, butter, egg, and peppermint extract in a bowl. Beat ingredients at medium speed until creamy.

3. Mix flour, baking powder, and salt. Add flour mixture and beat until well-combined.

4. Stir in crushed peppermint candy by hand. Refrigerate for one hour.

5. Preheat the oven to 350 degrees F. Crushed the remaining peppermint candies in the same method as the first time. Line baking sheets.

6. Shape chilled dough into ¾-inch balls and place on baking sheets about 2 inches apart.

7. Bake until edges are lightly browned. Cool cookies completely and store them in a container between pieces of parchment or wax paper.

Nutrition:

- Calories 150

- Carbohydrates 22 g

- Protein 2 g

- Sodium 67 mg

- Potassium 17 mg

- Phosphorus 24 mg

41.   Chocolate Chip Cookies

Preparation Time: 7 minutes

Cooking Time: 10 minutes

Servings: 10

Ingredients:

- 1/2 cup Semi-sweet chocolate chips

- 1/2 tsp. Baking soda

- 1/2 tsp. Vanilla

- 1 Egg

- 1 cup Flour

- 1/2 cup Margarine

- 4 tsp. Stevia

Directions:

1. Sift the dry ingredients.

2. Cream the margarine, stevia, vanilla, and egg with a whisk.

3. Add flour mixture and beat well.

4. Stir in the chocolate chips, then drop teaspoonfuls of the mixture over a greased baking sheet.

5. Bake for about 10 minutes at 375F.

6. Cool and serve.

Nutrition:

- Calories: 106.2

- Fat: 7g

- Carb: 8.9g

- Phosphorus: 19mg

- Potassium: 28mg

- Sodium: 98mg

- Protein: 1.5g

CHAPTER 14:

Salad Recipes

42. Cranberry Slaw

Preparation Time: 8 minutes

Cooking Time: 5 minutes

Servings: 4

Ingredients:

- 1/2 medium cabbage head, shredded

- 1 medium red apple, shredded

- 2 tablespoons onion, sliced

- 1/2 cup dried cranberries

- 1/4 cup almonds, toasted sliced

- 1/2 cup olive oil

- 1/4 teaspoon stevia

- 1/4 cup cider vinegar

- 1/2 tablespoon celery seed

- 1/2 teaspoon dry mustard

- 1/2 cup cream

Directions:

1. Take a suitable salad bowl.

2. Start tossing in all the ingredients.

3. Mix well and serve.

Nutrition:

- Calories 308

- Fat 24.5g

- Sodium 23mg

- Phosphorous 257mg

- Potassium 219mg

- Carbohydrate 13.5g

- Protein 2.6g

43.   Balsamic Beet Salad

Preparation Time: 10 minutes

Cooking Time: 0 minutes

Servings: 2

Ingredients:

- 1 cucumber, peeled and sliced

- 15 oz. canned low-sodium beets, sliced - 4 teaspoon balsamic vinegar

- 2 teaspoon sesame oil

- 2 tablespoons Gorgonzola cheese

Directions:

1. Take a suitable salad bowl.

2. Mix all the ingredients. Serve.

Nutrition:

- Calories 145 Fat 7.8g Sodium 426mgPhosphorus 79mg Potassium 229mg Carbohydrate 16.4g Protein 5g

CHAPTER 15:

Sauce Recipes

44.   Barbeque Sauce

Preparation Time: 10 minutes

Cooking time: 20 minutes

Servings: 8

Ingredients:

- 1/3 cup corn oil

- 1/2 cup tomato juice

- 1 tablespoon brown Swerve

- 1 garlic clove

- 1 tablespoon paprika

- 1/4 cup vinegar

- 1 teaspoon pepper

- 1/3 cup water

- 1/4 teaspoon onion powder

Directions:

1. Toss all the ingredients into a suitable saucepan.

2. Cook this sauce for 20 minutes with occasional stirring. Serve.

Nutrition:

- Calories 93 Fat 9.2g

- Carbohydrate 0.5g

- Protein 0.3g

- Sodium 42mg

- Potassium 68mg

- Phosphorous 31mg

45.   Apple Butter

Preparation Time: 5 minutes Cooking time: 2 hours

Servings: 20

Ingredients:

- 4 1/2 cups apple sauce

- 2 cups granulated Swerve

- 1/4 cup vinegar

- 1/2 teaspoon ground cloves

- 1/2 teaspoon cinnamon

Directions:

1. Whisk the apple sauce, Swerve, vinegar, ground cloves, and cinnamon in a small roasting pan.

2. Bake the mixture for 2 hours at 350 degrees F in a preheated oven until it thickens.

3. Mix well and transfer to a mason jar.

Nutrition: Calories 97 Fat 0g Carbohydrate 9.6g Protein 0.1g Sodium 1mg otassium 40mg Phosphorous 110mg

CHAPTER 16:

Vegetable Recipes

46.   Creamy Shells with Peas and Bacon

Preparation Time: 15 minutes

Cooking Time: 15 minutes

Servings: 4

Ingredients:

- 1 cup part-skim ricotta cheese

- ½ cup grated Parmesan cheese

- 3 slices bacon, cut into strips

- 1 cup onion, chopped

- ¾ cup of frozen green peas

- 1 tbsp. olive oil

- ¼ tsp. black pepper

- 3 garlic cloves, minced

- 3 cup cooked whole-wheat small shell pasta

- 1 tbsp. lemon juice

- 2 tbsp. unsalted butter

Directions:

1. Place ricotta, Parmesan cheese, butter, and pepper in a large bowl.

2. Cook bacon in a skillet until crisp. Set aside. Add the garlic and onion to the same skillet and fry until soft. Add to bowl with ricotta.

3. Cook the peas and add to the ricotta.

4. Add half a cup of the reserved cooking water and lemon juice to the ricotta mixture and mix well.

5. Add the pasta, bacon, and peas to the bowl and mix well.

6. Put freshly ground black pepper and serve.

Nutrition:

- Calories 429 Fat 14g

- Carbs 27g

- Protein 13g

- Sodium 244mg

- Potassium 172mg

- Phosphorous 203mg

47.   Double-Boiled Stewed Potatoes

Preparation Time: 20 minutes

Cooking Time: 30 minutes

Servings: 4

Ingredients:

- 2 cup potatoes, diced into ½ inch cubes

- ½ cup hot water

- ½ cup liquid non-dairy creamer

- ¼ tsp. garlic powder

- ¼ tsp. black pepper

- 2 tbsp. margarine

- 2 tsp. all-purpose white flour

Directions:

1. Soak or double boil the potatoes if you are on a low potassium diet.

2. Boil potatoes for 15 minutes.

3. Drain potatoes and return to pan. Put 1/2 cup of hot water, the creamer, garlic powder, pepper, and margarine. Heat to a boil.

4. Blend flour with a tablespoon of water, and then stir this into the potatoes.

5. Cook for 3 minutes until the mixture has thickened and the flour has cooked.

Nutrition:

- Calories 184

- Carbs 25g

- Protein 2g

- Potassium 161mg

- Phosphorous 65mg

48. Double-Boiled Country Style Fried Potatoes

Preparation Time: 20 minutes

Cooking Time: 20 minutes

Servings: 4

Ingredients:

- 2 medium potatoes, cut into large chips

- ½ cup canola oil

- ¼ tsp. ground cumin

- ¼ tsp. paprika

- ¼ tsp. white pepper

- 3 tbsp. ketchup

Directions:

1. Soak or double boil the potatoes if you are on a low potassium diet.

2. Heat oil over medium heat in a skillet.

3. Fry the potatoes for around 10 minutes until golden brown.

4. Drain potatoes, then sprinkle with cumin, pepper, and paprika.

5. Serve with ketchup or mayo.

Nutrition:

- Calories 156

- Fat 0.1g

- Carbs 21g

- Protein 2g

- Sodium 3mg

- Potassium 296mg

- Phosphorous 34mg

49.   Broccoli-Onion Latkes

Preparation Time: 15 minutes Cooking Time: 20 minutes

Servings: 4

Ingredients:

- 3 cups broccoli florets, diced

- ½ cup onion, chopped

- 2 large eggs, beaten

- 2 tbsp. all-purpose white flour

- 2 tbsp. olive oil

Directions:

1. Cook the broccoli for around 5 minutes until tender. Drain.

2. Mix the flour into the eggs. Combine the onion, broccoli, and egg mixture and stir through.

3. Prepare olive oil in a skillet on medium-high heat.

4. Drop a spoon of the mixture onto the pan to make 4 latkes. Cook each side until golden brown. Drain on a paper towel and serve.

Nutrition:

- Calories 140 Fat Carbs 7g Protein 6g Sodium 58mg Potassium 276mg Phosphorous 101mg

50.   Cranberry Cabbage

Preparation Time: 10 minutes Cooking Time: 20 minutes

Servings: 8

Ingredients:

- 10 ounces canned whole-berry cranberry sauce

- 1 tablespoon fresh lemon juice

- 1 medium head red cabbage

- 1/4 teaspoon ground cloves

Directions:

1. Place the cranberry sauce, lemon juice, and cloves in a large pan and bring to a boil.

2. Add the cabbage and reduce it to a simmer.

3. Cook until the cabbage is tender, occasionally stirring to make sure the sauce does not stick.

4. Delicious served with beef, lamb, or pork.

Nutrition:

- Calories 73 Fat 0g Carbs 18g Protein 1g

- Sodium 32mg Potassium 138mg Phosphorous 18mg

CHAPTER 17:

Meal Plan

D iets are easier when you have a definitive meal plan in your hands. This meal plan specifically for the renal diet will help you enjoy all the flavors and nutrients found in this cookbook easily. A proper renal diet can help you improve or maintain your kidney health by cutting down on the minerals that destabilize the internal balance of your kidneys: sodium, potassium, and phosphorus. This offers you the best possible renal diet recipes for everyday consumption ranging from breakfasts to side dishes, snacks, soups, salads, smoothies, meat, and desserts. Equipped with nutritional info and low sodium ingredients, each recipe is worth a try.

Week	Days	Breakfast	Lunch	Dinner
1	1	Raspberry Overnight Porridge	Tofu Stir Fry	Rosemary Grilled Chicken
	2	Egg White and Broccoli Omelet	Rosemary Grilled Chicken	Tasty Cold Cucumber Bisque
	3	Breakfast Maple Sausage	Carrot Casserole	Garlic-Paprika Chilean Sea Bass
	4	Egg and Veggie Muffins	Vegetable Minestrone	Quick and Easy Rice Pilaf

	5	American Blueberry Pancakes	Chicken Noodle Soup	Green Tuna Salad
	6	Mexican Scrambled Eggs in Tortilla	Grilled Corn on the Cob	Chicken and Savory Rice
	7	Bacon and Cheese Quiche	Couscous with Veggies	Cauliflower Rice
2	8	Raspberry Peach Breakfast Smoothie	Beef Stew with Apple Cider	Feta Bean Salad
	9	Spinach, Goat Cheese & Chorizo Omelet	Carrot-Apple Casserole	Beef Enchiladas
	10	Mexican Style Burritos	Beef Enchiladas	Tofu Soup
	11	Apple Cherry Breakfast Risotto	Ciabatta Rolls with Chicken Pesto	Creamy Pumpkin Soup
	12	Arugula Eggs with Chili Peppers	Green Pea Patties	Baked Macaroni & Cheese
	13	Berry Chia with Yogurt	Lasagna Rolls In Marinara Sauce	Herbed Soup with Black Beans

	14	Blueberry Muffins	Shrimp Quesadilla	Broccoli, Arugula, and Avocado Cream Soup
3	15	Fast Microwave Egg Scramble	Chicken Pineapple Curry	Vegetable Lentil Soup
	16	Mango Lassi Smoothie	Pizza Pitas	Taco Soup
	17	Shredded Chicken Chili	Cucumber Sandwich	Kale Slaw
	18	Buckwheat and Grapefruit Porridge	Steak with Onion	Ground Beef and Rice Soup
	19	Bulgur, Couscous, and Buckwheat Cereal	Turkey Pinwheels	Spicy Veggie Pancakes
	20	Berries and Cream Breakfast Cake	Crispy Lemon Chicken	Roasted Asparagus
	21	Hot Fruit Salad	Chicken Tacos	Chicken Pho
4	22	Summer Veggie Omelet	Baked Pork Chops	Mashed Peas

23	Eggplant Chicken Sandwich	Mexican Chorizo Sausage	Chicken Paella
24	Yogurt Parfait with Strawberries	Chicken Paella	Creamy Broccoli Soup
25	Turkey and Spinach Scramble on Melba Toast	Lettuce Wraps with Chicken	Pesto Pasta Salad
26	Creamy Keto Cucumber Salad	Beef Kabobs with Pepper	Sweet Glazed Salmon
27	Spinach and Ham Frittata	Tuna Twist	Pork Souvlaki
28	Tasty Beef and Liver Burger	Pork Souvlaki	Asparagus Fried Rice

Kitchen Staples

Spices and Herbs

- Oregano

- Thyme

- Onion powder

- Garlic powder

- Paprika

- Cayenne pepper

- Black pepper

- Chili powder

- Cumin

- Basil

- Rosemary

Vegetables

- Onion

- Garlic

- Carrots

- Celery

- Bell peppers

- Beets

- Cucumbers

- Peas

Fruits

- Apples

- Pineapples

- Blueberries

- Strawberries

- Raspberries

- Cranberries

- Banana

Meat and Poultry

- Pork chops

- Beef Briskets

- Chicken legs

- Chicken breasts

- Turkey breasts

- Oysters

Dairy and Non-Diary Items

- Yogurt

- Cheese

- Low-Fat milk

- Rice milk

Miscellaneous

- Chia seeds

- Flour

- Sesame seeds(black and white)

- Sesame oil

- Olive oil

- Cherry pie filling

- Pie Crusts

- Green beans

- Butter

- Sweet sauce

- Hot sauce

- Splenda

- Oyster crackers

- Tortilla

- Low sodium bouillon cubes

- Wild rice

- Eggs

Conclusion

When you are diagnosed with renal disease, it is perfectly natural and common to have some questions regarding kidney function and renal diet. The exact amount of protein you should take per day depends on your current body weight, renal disease stage, and general health status. This is something that you can figure out with your doctor or renal dietitian. However, in most cases, doctors recommend approximately 1.1-1.3 gr of protein per kg of body weight daily. For example, if you weigh 143Pounds/65Kg, you can eat up to 84 grams of protein per day without any problems.

Since many nutrient-dense foods should be avoided in a renal diet because of their high potassium or phosphorus content, it is generally suggested to take water-soluble vitamins. These are B-complex vitamins and vitamin C in smaller doses. However, excess supplementation may lead to side effects like stomach irritation, gas, and constipation, making sure you do not exceed the daily-recommended amount on the package.

Drinks that contain lower amounts of alcohol than others, e.g., wine and beer, are fine to drink on a semi-regular basis, e.g., 2-3 times a week. However, heavy alcoholic drinks like vodka, rum, tequila, gin, and whiskey should be limited to 2-3 times a month, as frequent consumption will place kidneys and other vital organs under stress.

When you are checking a product label or new recipe but don't know if it's low in potassium or not, here is a basic guideline of levels per Serving:

- Very low potassium levels up to 35 mg/serving

- Low potassium levels up to 150 mg/serving

- Moderate potassium levels between 150-250 mg/serving

- High potassium levels 250-500 mg/serving

- Very high potassium levels 500mg+/serving

If you are checking a recipe, make sure that you calculate all ingredients' total levels to determine the amount of potassium. This made it easier for you by including low or moderate recipes in potassium and displaying the actual potassium level per serving. These recipes are ideal for whether you have been diagnosed with a kidney problem or want to prevent any kidney issue.

A limitation of fluids is generally recommended during the last stages of kidney damage, and it would be better to discuss it with your doctor. If you go the opposite and only drink 500ml of fluids or less per day, you risk dehydrating yourself and cause other problems.

Artificial sweeteners that are low in carbs are generally acceptable to the consumer within the renal diet except for aspartame, which is linked to many health problems. Sweeteners like stevia, sucralose, and xylitol are perfectly fine when consumed moderately regularly.